T0113874

-

THE BLESSING OF THE LORD WILL MAKE YOU RICH

Lifestyles of the Bible's
RICH AND FAMOUS

Sue Ann Szczech

WESTBOW
PRESS®
A DIVISION OF THOMAS NELSON
& ZONDERVAN

This book is a work of non-fiction. Unless otherwise noted, the author and the publisher make no explicit guarantees as to the accuracy of the information contained in this book and in some cases, names of people and places have been altered to protect their privacy.

WestBow Press books may be ordered through booksellers or by contacting:

WestBow Press
A Division of Thomas Nelson & Zondervan
1663 Liberty Drive
Bloomington, IN 47403
www.westbowpress.com
844-714-3454

Scripture taken from the King James Version of the Bible.

ISBN: 978-1-6642-5985-0 (sc)
ISBN: 978-1-6642-5984-3 (e)

Print information available on the last page.

WestBow Press rev. date: 12/08/2022

TABLE OF CONTENTS

Thus says the LORD, your Redeemer, the Holy One of Israel: "I *am* the LORD your God, Who teaches you to profit, Who leads you by the way you should go. Isaiah 48:17

PREFACE

The blessing of the Lord makes one rich, and He adds no sorrow with it. Proverbs 10:22

The blessing of the LORD brings wealth, without painful toil for it. Proverbs 10:22 NIV

I chose this scripture as the title of this book because it describes just what the book is about. With the Lord's blessing, we will be rich with no sorrow added with it.

The Blessing of the Lord, in the Hebrew means prosperity. The dictionary meaning of prosperity means the condition of being successful or thriving; *especially*: economic well being.

Rich, in the Hebrew means to accumulate and to grow or make rich. To make self rich, or make Kings.

And He added no sorrow with it, in the Hebrew sorrow means *painful toil*. So, in other words, the Lord wants to bless us without it being painful and toiling work. The Lord speaks in Deuteronomy about giving the Israelites great and beautiful cities which they did not build, and houses full of all good things which they did not fill, and wells which they did not dig, and vineyards and olive trees which they did not plant. That pretty much sums it up…having the blessing of the Lord will make you rich without making it grievous, but making it easy.

INTRODUCTION

The lord wants to bless us so we can be a blessing to others and not walk away from hungry and hurting people.

In the parable of the Good Samaritan, the gospel of Luke 10:25-37, the lawyer asked Jesus how to obtain eternal life. Jesus asked him what the law said. And he said, to love the Lord your God with all your heart, soul, strength and mind, and to love your neighbor as yourself. Jesus said that was correct. Then the lawyer asked who is my neighbor? Jesus replied and told him a parable about a man who was robbed and beat up and left for dead on the side of the road. A Priest and a Levite passed by and did not pay any attention to him. Then the Good Samaritan passed by and helped him by cleaning him up and bringing him to a hotel to stay until he was well and gave the inn keeper money in advance for anything that the man needed, and if there was any more money owing he would pay the inn keeper when he returned.

Would you be willing, and in the position to help the wounded man on the side of the road or would you just walk on by?

Another important reason is that there are so many people that have the wrong perception of what God would want for us.

People talk about the fact that Ministers of the Gospel should not be rich, or shouldn't talk about finances, or giving. Also, that Christians shouldn't be rich or have too much money. Why not? Why can everyone else in the world be rich, but not the Ministers of the Lord, or Christians? It says in the Bible that the Lord says the silver is mine and the gold is mine, and everything in the earth is His. So if that is true, which it is, because He created the world and everything in it, and we are called his children, by Him, then we are heirs and have what He has.

In so many areas of the Bible, God is said to be our Father. In this natural world a good loving father only wants the best for us. He wants us to be successful in everything we do. Fathers want us to go to college or learn a trade so that we can have a good life and have money for our families. So we can have good things like houses and cars etc. Can you actually picture a loving father wanting his children to be poor, living on welfare and in government housing, saying oh son, I am so happy you are poor, I hope you get poorer? He doesn't want us to be sick, he doesn't want us to be poor, and he wants us to be successful, knowledgeable, and happy.

In the Bible it says, how much more does our Heavenly Father want for us, whose love is perfect toward us.

If you then, being evil, know how to give good gifts unto your children, how much more shall your Father, who is in heaven, give good things to them that ask Him? Math 7:11

This book is meant to help you see how God has blessed men and women throughout the Bible in their lives and their finances, and how He wants you to be blessed also. And we will conclude with the characteristics it takes for us to prosper. They were of course blessed by the Lord in every area, but we will focus on the finances.

CHAPTER 1
ABRAHAM

Now the Lord had said to Abram; "Get out of your country, from your family and from your father's house, to a land that I will show you. I will make you a great nation; I will bless you and make your name great; and you shall be a blessing. I will bless those who bless you, and I will curse him who curses you; and in you all the families of the earth shall be blessed." Genesis 12:1-3

First of all, God is telling Abram to move, from his family, to a new place that the Lord will show him. And if Abram is obedient and listens to what God says to do, God will *bless* him with prosperity. The word blessed, in the Hebrew, means God wants to congratulate Abram and make him a *blessing* or to make him prosperous.

Lot also, who went with Abram, had flocks and herds and tents. Now the land was not able to support them that they might dwell together, for their possessions were so great that they could not dwell together. Gen 13: 5,6

Their increase was so great that they had to separate and go to different areas and lands!

So he said, "I *am* Abraham's servant. The LORD has blessed my master greatly, and he has become great; and He has given him flocks and herds, silver and gold, male and female servants, and camels and donkeys. And Sarah my master's wife bore a son to my master when she was old; and to him he has given all that he has." Gen 24:34-36

Now that Abraham was getting old he gave everything to his son. The Lord gave Abraham wealth and riches, and now it was handed down to his son Isaac. But going forward you will see that God blessed Isaac also because he listened to the Lord and did what He said.

And Abraham gave all that he had to Isaac. Gen 25:5

Isaac didn't have to do anything, just inherit it from His Father. (Wealth and riches with no sorrow added to it, without painful toiling!) Yes, that does sometimes happen where money is handed down from generations, but if it is not handled correctly it can go away very quickly. As in the case of the Prodigal Son where he asked for his inheritance before his father died and went out into the world and spent it foolishly. Going forward you will see that God blessed Isaac, not just because he was Abraham's son, in the natural, but because he listened to what God said to do, to place him in a position to be wealthy.

If someone told you to go to a certain city and there you would find a million dollars waiting for you, would you go? Most of the time God is not always that specific, He usually requires us to take a first step sometimes not really knowing what will happen or how it will work out. As we take the first step, each step is revealed to us as we trust Him with all our heart.

CHAPTER 2
ISAAC

There was a famine in the land, besides the first famine that was in the days of Abraham.

> Then the LORD appeared to him and said: "Do not go down to Egypt; live in the land of which I shall tell you. Dwell in this land, and I will be with you and bless you; for to you and your descendants I give all these lands, and I will perform the oath which I swore to Abraham your father. And I will make your descendants multiply as the stars of heaven; I will give to your descendants all these lands; and in your seed all the nations of the earth shall be blessed; because Abraham obeyed My voice and kept My charge, My commandments, My statutes, and My laws. "Genesis 26:1-5

> Then Isaac sowed in that land, and received in the same year a hundredfold; and the Lord blessed him. Genesis 26:12

Remember, there was a famine in the land, and he went where the Lord told him to go.

The man began to prosper, and continued prospering until he became very prosperous; for he had possessions of flocks and possessions of herds and a great number of servants. So the Philistines envied him. Genesis 26:13-14

The people around him envied him because the Lord blessed him greatly!

Abimelech said unto Isaac, go from us; for you are much mightier than us. Genesis 26:16

And the Lord appeared to Isaac in the night, and said, I am the God of Abraham, your father; fear not, for I am with you, and will bless you, and multiply your seed for my servant Abraham's sake. Genesis 26:24

God was saying to him not to be afraid, I am with you even though you have to leave that area, I will bless you and multiply your seed.

CHAPTER 3
JACOB

Jacob was borne by Isaac and had a family and was living with his father in law, Laban. He worked and served him for many years.

> And it came to pass, when Rachel had borne Joseph, that Jacob said to Laban, "Send me away, that I may go to my own place and to my country." Genesis 30:25

> And Laban said to him, "Please *stay*, if I have found favor in your eyes, *for* I have learned by experience that the LORD has blessed me for your sake." Then he said, "Name me your wages, and I will give *it*." Genesis 30:27, 28

> So *Jacob* said to him, "You know how I have served you and how your livestock has been with me. For what you had before I *came was* little, and it has increased to a great amount; the LORD has blessed you since my coming. And now, when shall I also provide for my own house?" Genesis 30:29, 30

The Lord increased Laban for Jacob's sake, because Jacob worked for him. The Lord will prosper everything that you will put your hand to, your business or the business that you work for!

> **And God said to him, "Your name *is* Jacob; your name shall not be called Jacob anymore, but Israel shall be your name." So He called his name Israel. Also God said to him: "I *am* God Almighty. Be fruitful and multiply; a nation and a company of nations shall proceed from you, and kings shall come from your body. Genesis 35:10, 11**

Being a King is definitely a blessing from the Lord!

CHAPTER 4
JOSEPH

Now Israel loved Joseph more than all his children, because he *was* the son of his old age. Also he made him a tunic of *many* colors. But when his brothers saw that their father loved him more than all his brothers, they hated him and could not speak peaceably to him. Genesis 37:3, 4

So, they threw him in a pit and then sold him to the Ishmaelites. They brought back Joseph's bloody coat to his father and said that they found it and Joseph was gone. Joseph ended up in Egypt with Potiphar, an officer of Pharaoh's, and captain of the guard.

The Lord was with Joseph, and he was a successful man; and he was in the house of his master the Egyptian. And his master saw that the Lord *was* with him and that the Lord made all he did to prosper in his hand. So Joseph found favor in his sight, and served him. Then he made him overseer of his house, and all *that* he had he put under his authority. So it was, from the time *that* he had made him overseer of his house and all that he had, that the Lord blessed the Egyptian's house for Joseph's

sake; and the blessing of the LORD was on all that he had in the house and in the field. **Genesis 39:2-6**

Now Joseph was handsome in form and appearance. Potiphar's wife cast her eyes upon Joseph and wanted to lie with him. He refused to compromise, so she caught him by his garment, saying lie with me: and he left his garment in her hand, and fled and got out. She then proceeded to blame him for trying to seduce her and Joseph ended up in Jail.

But the LORD was with Joseph and showed him mercy, and He gave him favor in the sight of the keeper of the prison. And the keeper of the prison committed to Joseph's hand all the prisoners who *were* in the prison; whatever they did there, it was his doing. The keeper of the prison did not look into anything *that was* under *Joseph's* authority, because the LORD was with him; and whatever he did, the LORD made *it* prosper. Genesis 39:21-23

So, everything that Joseph put his hand to prospered, and anyone that Joseph worked with could see the blessing of the Lord on him and knew that they were blessed because he was blessed. The reason: Joseph loved, honored, and obeyed the Lord.

If you are familiar at all with the story of Joseph, he ultimately ends up being the Pharaoh's right hand man, serving directly under him as the Ruler over all the land of Egypt. Why? Because the Lord gave Joseph the interpretation of a dream Pharaoh had and saved Egypt from a great famine. And, which ultimately saved all of Joseph's family from being affected also. The blessing of the Lord brought Joseph from prison, to suddenly, in one day, being the ruler over a country and region. Hmm... The blessing of the Lord will do that for you also, because the Lord is no respecter of persons.

Joseph's blessing from the Lord was wisdom to interpret dreams. When Joseph had finished interpreting the dream for Pharaoh, the Lord also gave Joseph wisdom for the plan to store all the food for the first seven years of plenty, so there would be no lack the seven years of famine.

> Then Pharaoh said to Joseph, "Inasmuch as God has shown you all this, *there is* no one as discerning and wise as you. You shall be over my house, and all my people shall be ruled according to your word; only in regard to the throne will I be greater than you." And Pharaoh said to Joseph, "See, I have set you over all the land of Egypt."

> Then Pharaoh took his signet ring off his hand and put it on Joseph's hand; and he clothed him in garments of fine linen and put a gold chain around his neck. And he had him ride in the second chariot which he had; and they cried out before him, "Bow the knee!" So he set him over all the land of Egypt. Pharaoh also said to Joseph, "I *am* Pharaoh, and without your consent no man may lift his hand or foot in all the land of Egypt." And Pharaoh called Joseph's name Zaphnath-Paaneah. And he gave him as a wife Asenath, the daughter of Poti-Pherah priest of On. So Joseph went out over *all* the land of Egypt. Gen 41:39-45

The blessing of the Lord, it maketh rich, and He added no sorrow with it.

CHAPTER 5
JOSHUA

Joshua took over after Moses died in bringing the Israelites to the Promised Land. He obeyed God in conquering the lands that God had prepared for them. It didn't always look easy, that is why the Lord is encouraging him in the following verses. But he was saying that the conquering would be well worth it.

After the death of Moses the servant of the LORD, it came to pass that the LORD spoke to Joshua the son of Nun, Moses' assistant, saying: Moses My servant is dead. Now therefore, arise, go over this Jordan, you and all this people, to the land which I am giving to them—the children of Israel. Every place that the sole of your foot will tread upon I have given you, as I said to Moses. From the wilderness and this Lebanon as far as the great river, the River Euphrates, all the land of the Hittites, and to the Great Sea toward the going down of the sun, shall be your territory. No man shall *be able to* stand before you all the days of your life; as I was with Moses, *so* I will be with you. I will not leave you nor forsake you. Be strong and of good courage, for to this people you shall divide as an inheritance the land which I swore to their fathers to give them. Joshua 1:1-6

Then the Lord continues to say….

Only be strong and very courageous, that you may observe to do according to all the law which Moses My servant commanded you; do not turn from it to the right hand or to the left, that you may prosper wherever you go. Joshua 1:7

(Notice how he says be strong and very courageous so you can obey, because the devil will try to bring things against you to discourage you from obeying. For example, fear and fear of man.)

This Book of the Law shall not depart from your mouth, but you shall meditate in it day and night, that you may observe to do according to all that is written in it. For then you will make your way prosperous, and then you will have good success. Have I not commanded you? Be strong and of good courage; do not be afraid, nor be dismayed, for the Lord your God *is* with you wherever you go. Joshua 1:8,9

Knowing the word in your heart will cause you to obey the word and then you will be prosperous and successful.

Have I not commanded you?? Wow, it sounds like the Lord really means business. He is commanding us not to be afraid and to trust Him because He will always be with us. And to believe He will give us the best that He has.

I have given you a land for which you did not labor, and cities which you did not build, and you dwell

in them; you eat of the vineyards and olive groves which you did not plant. Joshua 24:13

Now at the end of the book of Joshua they have conquered and divided the land amongst themselves and the Lord gave them Lands which they didn't have to labor for and cities which they didn't have to build, and vineyards and olive yards which they didn't have to plant. Well, that's sounds like **<u>rich, with no sorrow added to it.</u>**

CHAPTER 6
RUTH

Ruth is a story about a Moabite woman whose husband died, and left her with her mother in law, an Israelite in the land of Moab. Her mother in law, Naomi, decided to go back to Israel to her hometown and relatives. Ruth made the decision to go with her on her journey, even though Naomi advised her to stay with her relatives and in her hometown. Ruth insisted on staying with Naomi and was faithful to Naomi and the Lord. When they returned to Israel Ruth found work to support Naomi and herself and was unknowingly working for a relative of Naomi, named Boaz.

Well, in the end the Lord blessed Ruth by marrying Boaz who was wealthy and had a business. They had a child and named him Jesse who was King David's father. And of course you may know that Jesus came out of this lineage. So it sounds like the Lord blessed Ruth greatly and in many ways for being faithful to Him and Naomi.

CHAPTER 7
HANNAH

This story is not particularly about finances, but it is about a woman who cried out to the Lord from her heart and the Lord blessed her with a child. It seems that whatever it is that we want. If we are desperate enough for it, He hears our prayers. Having children isn't necessarily a need, just as being rich is not either, but a blessing from the Lord.

> Now there was a certain man of Ramathaim Zophim, of the mountains of Ephraim, and his name *was* Elkanah. And he had two wives: the name of one *was* Hannah, and the name of the other Peninnah. Peninnah had children, but Hannah had no children. This man went up from his city yearly to worship and sacrifice to the Lord of hosts in Shiloh. And whenever the time came for Elkanah to make an offering, he would give portions to Peninnah his wife and to all her sons and daughters. But to Hannah he would give a double portion, for he loved Hannah, although the Lord had closed her womb. And her rival also provoked her severely, to make her miserable, because the Lord had closed her womb. So it was, year by year, when she went

up to the house of the Lord, that she provoked her; therefore she wept and did not eat.

Hannah's Vow

Then Elkanah her husband said to her, "Hannah, why do you weep? Why do you not eat? And why is your heart grieved? *Am* I not better to you than ten sons?"

So Hannah arose after they had finished eating and drinking in Shiloh. Now Eli the priest was sitting on the seat by the doorpost of the tabernacle of the Lord. And she *was* in bitterness of soul, and prayed to the Lord and wept in anguish. Then she made a vow and said, "O Lord of hosts, if You will indeed look on the affliction of Your maidservant and remember me, and not forget Your maidservant, but will give Your maidservant a male child, then I will give him to the Lord all the days of his life, and no razor shall come upon his head."

And it happened, as she continued praying before the Lord, that Eli watched her mouth. Now Hannah spoke in her heart; only her lips moved, but her voice was not heard. Therefore, Eli thought she was drunk. So Eli said to her, "How long will you be drunk? Put your wine away from you!"

But Hannah answered and said, "No, my lord, I *am* a woman of sorrowful spirit. I have drunk neither wine nor intoxicating drink, but have poured out my soul before the Lord. "Do not consider your maidservant a wicked woman, for out of the abundance of my complaint and grief I have spoken until now."

Then Eli answered and said, "Go in peace, and the God of Israel grant your petition which you have asked of Him."

And she said, "Let your maidservant find favor in your sight." So the woman went her way and ate, and her face was no longer *sad*. 1 Samuel 1-18

So it came to pass in the process of time that Hannah conceived and bore a son, and called his name Samuel, saying, "Because I have asked for him from the Lord." 1 Samuel 1:20

Hannah poured out her soul to the Lord, and wept bitterly. Eli the priest thought she was drunk; she was so desperate. The Lord is a rewarder of them that diligently seek Him. The Lord heard her cry and within a short amount of time, probably nine months she bore a son.

The reason I chose the story of Hannah is because whatever we desire or ask of the Lord, and depending upon our motive and how serious we are, is the way we will receive our answer. The effectual fervent prayer of a righteous man will avail much. Hannah gave Samuel to the Church and he grew up to be a prophet of the Lord.

The Lord then blessed Hannah with three sons and two daughters.

CHAPTER 8
ELIHAH AND THE
WIDOW WOMAN

Now there was a drought in the land and God spoke to Elijah and told him to go to the brook Cherith, and that he shall drink from the brook, and God would also command the ravens to feed him there. So he did as the Lord told him and the Lord sent ravens to feed him bread and flesh in the morning and bread and flesh in the evening, and he drank from the brook.

After a while the brook dried up because there had been no rain in the land. So the Lord told him to go to Zarephath and told him that He had commanded a widow woman to sustain him there.

When he came to the city there was a woman there gathering sticks, he called to her and asked her to fetch him some water in a vessel for him to drink. And as she was going to get it, he asked her to also bring him a morsel of bread. She said to Elijah, as the Lord lives, I do not have a cake, but a handful of meal in a barrel and a little oil in a cruse; I am gathering two sticks so that I may go in and prepare it for me and my son, so that we may eat it and die.

And Elijah said to her, "Do not fear; go *and* do as you have said, but make me a small cake from it first, and bring *it* to me; and afterward make *some* for yourself and your son. For thus says the

LORD God of Israel: 'The meal in the barrel shall not be used up, nor shall the cruse of oil run dry, until the day the LORD sends rain on the earth.'" So she went away and did according to the word of Elijah; and she and he and her household ate for *many* days. The meal in the barrel was not used up, nor did the cruse of oil run dry, according to the word of the LORD which He spoke by Elijah. 1 Kings 17:13-16

Now at one point Elijah may have thought he missed it from God, going to a woman who basically had nothing. But if everyone does the will of God and stays obedient to His word, the blessings will flow. And that they did, the meal in the barrel never failed and the cruse of oil never ran dry until the drought was over and it rained on the land. Wow, a continual miracle of provision!

CHAPTER 9
THE WIDOWS OIL

This is a short but powerful story of how the Lord blessed a woman whose husband died and left her with a large amount of debt. She cried out to God and He showed up.

A certain woman of the wives of the sons of the prophets cried out to Elisha, saying, "Your servant my husband is dead, and you know that your servant feared the LORD. And the creditor is coming to take my two sons to be his slaves."

So Elisha said to her, "What shall I do for you? Tell me, what do you have in the house?" And she said, "Your maidservant has nothing in the house but a jar of oil."

Then he said, "Go, borrow vessels from everywhere, from all your neighbors—empty vessels; do not gather just a few. And when you have come in, you shall shut the door behind you and your sons; then pour it into all those vessels, and set aside the full ones."

So she went from him and shut the door behind her and her sons, who brought *the vessels* to her; and she poured *it* out. Now it came to pass, when the vessels were full, that she said to her son, "Bring me another vessel."

And he said to her, "*There is* not another vessel." So the oil ceased. Then she came and told the man of God. And he said, "Go, sell the oil and pay your debt; and you *and* your sons live on the rest." 2 Kings 4:1-7

HALLELUJIAH!!! That is awesome! The Lord gave her an oil business and when she was sold out she paid her debt and was able to live on the rest!! Wow! God is good! God blessed her and with no sorrow added to it!

CHAPTER 10
HEZEKIAH

Hezekiah began to reign as King of Judah. He did all that was right in the sight of the Lord, according to all that his father David did.

He removed the pagan shrines, smashed the sacred pillars, and cut down the Asherah poles. He broke up the bronze serpent that Moses had made, because the people of Israel had been offering sacrifices to it.

Hezekiah trusted in the Lord, the God of Israel. There was no one like him among all the kings of Judah, either before or after his time. He remained faithful to the Lord in everything, and he carefully obeyed all the commands the Lord had given Moses. So the Lord was with him, and Hezekiah was successful in everything he did. 2 Kings 18:3-7 NLT

Soon after this, the king of Babylon sent Hezekiah his best wishes and a gift, for he had heard that Hezekiah had been very sick. Hezekiah received the Babylonian envoys and showed them everything in his treasure houses—the silver, the gold, the spices, and the aromatic oils. He also took them to

see his armory and showed them everything in his royal treasuries. 2 Kings 20:12,13

Hmm, it's sounds like he is rich....

Hezekiah is another example of a King that remained faithful and obedient to the Lord God, and God blessed him with treasure houses!!

CHAPTER 11
KING DAVID

Now therefore, thus shall you say to my servant David, thus says the LORD of hosts: "I took you from the sheepfold, from following the sheep, to be ruler over My people, over Israel. And I have been with you wherever you have gone, and have cut off all your enemies from before you, and have made you a great name, like the name of the great men who *are* on the earth. 2 Samuel 7:8,9.

David was thirty years old when he began to reign and he reigned forty years. In Hebron he reigned over Judah seven years and six months, and in Jerusalem he reigned thirty and three years over all Israel and Judah. 2 Samuel 5:4,5.

David grew greater and greater; for the Lord of Hosts was with him. 1 Chronicles 11:9

And the fame of David went out into all lands; and the Lord brought the fear of him upon all nations. 1 Chronicles 14:17

**And David behaved himself wisely in all his ways;
and the LORD was with him. 1 Samuel 18:14**

David was very committed and faithful to the Lord, and he trusted in the Lord with all his heart. One of the examples is David and Goliath, David had such a faith and trust in God, that he took on the giant Goliath as a youth knowing that God would back him up and help him overcome Goliath and his nation.

David did not start out necessarily prosperous, in the monetary sense, but in the end was very wealthy.

In 1 Samuel 18:22-23, when King Saul wanted David to marry his daughter, Michal, he sent his servants to speak to David.

David replied, do you think it is a small matter to become the King's son-in-law? I am only a poor man and little known. David was saying he was too poor to take Michal as his bride. Normally a bride-price was paid by the bridegroom to the father of the bride. Saul said that he wants no other price for the bride than one hundred Philistines foreskins. David went out and got two hundred foreskins and brought them to Saul, who was hoping that David wouldn't come back and would be killed. Saul then knew that God was with David, and became still more afraid of him, and he remained his enemy the rest of his days.

The Philistine commanders continued to go out to battle, and as often as they did, David met with more success than the rest of Saul's officers, and his name became well known. God's favor and blessing was on David.

David was being pursued and hunted by Saul and living in caves and the wilderness for many years hoping not to be killed. David had the opportunity to kill Saul several times but didn't touch him. He respected and loved him no matter what Saul did to him. He would not touch the Lord's anointed.

So when King Saul died, David was a free man in a sense, not having to flee or run any more, but probably didn't have a lot of finances or assets to work with. He was then appointed King over Judah and Israel.

David also found refuge in the Lord continuously as we see written in the Psalms, as he fought for his life in the wilderness, and as with all the trials and circumstances he went through he looked to the Lord for his help. So David found at an early age that God was his refuge, help and salvation and loved the Lord with all his heart.

In Psalm 118 David cried out to God and said send prosperity now!!! That was at the beginning of David's reign as king. At the end of King David's reign, he gave almost as much as the whole congregation when giving for the building of the Temple. His offering was 3000 talents of Gold and 7000 talents of refined silver. In our terms that would be well over 1 billion dollars! And, I believe, David had a heart where he would be willing to give all of it, if the Lord asked him. That is why the Lord blessed him. So the Lord blessed King David, and he died in a good old age, full of days, riches and honor; and Solomon his son reigned in his stead.

> Now, my son, may the LORD be with you; and may you prosper, and build the house of the LORD your God, as He has said to you. Only may the LORD give you wisdom and understanding, and give you charge concerning Israel, that you may keep the law of the LORD your God. Then you will prosper, if you take care to fulfill the statutes and judgments with which the LORD charged Moses concerning Israel. Be strong and of good courage; do not fear nor be dismayed. 1 Chronicles 22:11-13

> Now the days of David drew near that he should die, and he charged Solomon his son, saying: "I go the way of all the earth; be strong, therefore, and prove yourself a man. And keep the charge of the LORD your God: to walk in His ways, to keep His statutes, His commandments, His judgments, and

His testimonies, as it is written in the Law of Moses, that you may prosper in all that you do and wherever you turn; that the LORD may fulfill His word which He spoke concerning me, saying, 'If your sons take heed to their way, to walk before Me in truth with all their heart and with all their soul,' He said, 'you shall not lack a man on the throne of Israel.' 1 Kings 2:1-4

CHAPTER 12
KING SOLOMON

Solomon sat on the throne of the Lord instead of David his father, and prospered; and all Israel obeyed him. 1 Chronicles 29:23

And the Lord magnified Solomon exceedingly in the sight of all Israel, and bestowed upon him such royal majesty as had not been on any king before him in Israel. 1 Chronicles 29:25

Now Solomon the son of David was strengthened in his kingdom, and the Lord his God *was* with him and exalted him exceedingly. 2 Chronicles 1:1

Then God said to Solomon: "Because this was in your heart, and you have not asked riches or wealth or honor or the life of your enemies, nor have you asked long life—but have asked wisdom and knowledge for yourself, that you may judge My people over whom I have made you king— *wisdom and knowledge are granted to you; and I will give you riches and wealth and honor, such as none of the kings have had who were before you, nor shall any after you have the like.*" 2 Chronicles 1:11.12

Hmm…God is definitely blessing Solomon!!

THE QUEEN OF SHEBA

Now when the queen of Sheba heard of the fame of Solomon, she came to Jerusalem to test Solomon with hard questions, *having* a very great retinue, camels that bore spices, gold in abundance, and precious stones; and when she came to Solomon, she spoke with him about all that was in her heart. So Solomon answered all her questions; there was nothing so difficult for Solomon that he could not explain it to her. And when the queen of Sheba had seen the wisdom of Solomon, the house that he had built, the food on his table, the seating of his servants, the service of his waiters and their apparel, his cupbearers and their apparel, and his entryway by which he went up to the house of the LORD, there was no more spirit in her.

Then she said to the king: "*It was* a true report which I heard in my own land about your words and your wisdom. However, I did not believe their words until I came and saw with my own eyes; and indeed the half of the greatness of your wisdom was not told me. You exceed the fame of which I heard. Happy *are* your men and happy *are* your servants, who stand continually before you and hear your wisdom! Blessed be the LORD your God, who delights in you, setting you on His throne *to be* king for the LORD your God! Because your God has loved Israel, to establish them forever, therefore He made you king over them, to do justice and righteousness."

And she gave the king one hundred and twenty talents of gold, spices in great abundance, and precious stones; there never were any spices such as those the queen of Sheba gave to King Solomon. 2 Chronicles 9: 1-9

Solomon was rich because God gave him wisdom, knowledge and understanding!

The weight of gold that came to Solomon yearly was six hundred and sixty-six talents of gold, (which in our terms would be well over 900 million annually), not including *what* the traveling merchants and traders brought. And all the kings of Arabia and governors of the country brought gold and silver to Solomon. 2 Chronicles 9:13, 14

All King Solomon's drinking vessels *were* gold and all the vessels of the House of the Forest of Lebanon *were* pure gold. Not *one was* silver, for this was accounted as nothing in the days of Solomon. For the king's ships went to Tarshish with the servants of Hiram. Once every three years the merchant ships came, bringing gold, silver, ivory, apes, and monkeys. 2 Chronicles 9:20, 21

Solomon had four thousand stalls for horses and chariots and twelve thousand horsemen whom he stationed in the chariot cities and with the king at Jerusalem. 2 Chronicles 9:25

Solomon accumulated chariots and horses; he had fourteen hundred chariots and twelve thousand horses. The king made silver and gold as common in Jerusalem as stones, and cedar as plentiful as sycamore-fig trees in the foothills.

So King Solomon surpassed all the kings of the earth in riches and wisdom. And all the kings of the earth sought the presence of Solomon to hear his wisdom, which God had put in his heart. Each man brought his present: articles of silver and gold, garments, armor, spices, horses, and mules, at a set rate year by year. 2 Chronicles 9:22-24

And God gave Solomon wisdom and exceedingly great understanding, and largeness of heart like the sand on the seashore. Thus Solomon's wisdom excelled the wisdom of all the men of the East and all the wisdom of Egypt. For he was wiser than all men— and his fame was in all the surrounding nations. He spoke three thousand proverbs, and his songs were one thousand and five. Also he spoke of trees, from the cedar tree of Lebanon even to the hyssop that springs out of the wall; he spoke also of animals, of birds, of creeping things, and of fish. And men of all nations, from all the kings of the earth who had heard of his wisdom, came to hear the Wisdom of Solomon. 1 Kings 4:29-34

People would come to Solomon to hear his wisdom regarding each man's situation or just general wisdom and teaching. That is what brought him riches and honor and favor, like no other King.

Solomon reigned in Jerusalem over all Israel forty years. Then Solomon rested with his fathers, and was buried in the City of David his father. And Rehoboam his son reigned in his place. 2 Chronicles 9:30, 31

CHAPTER 13
QUEEN ESTHER

The Book of Esther is about a Jewish man named Mordecai and his cousin Esther. They were under the rule of King Ahasuerus of Persia; they originally had been taken captive under the rule of King Nebuchadnezzar of Babylon. They were descendants of the tribe of Benjamin. Mordecai was working for King Ahasuerus in his administration.

The story of Esther starts with King Ahasuerus having a feast and eventually calling for his wife Queen Vashti to come and join him. But she denies his request and refuses to come. So the king was very angry and asked his advisors what he should do. They advised the king to get rid of her because then all the country would see that she could be disrespectful to the king and the wives would do likewise to their husbands. The king agreed with them and they also advised to have a group of virgin women groomed and beautified for the king to choose a new Queen. Esther was chosen to be one of those women. Esther was highly favored everywhere she went. She was very well favored by the man in charge of the chosen women and he gave Esther seven servants to help her.

Now the young woman pleased him, and she obtained his favor; so he readily gave beauty preparations to her, besides her allowance. Then seven choice maidservants were provided for her from the king's palace, and he moved her and her maidservants to the best *place* in the house of the women.

> Esther had not revealed her people or family, for Mordecai had charged her not to reveal *it*. And every day Mordecai paced in front of the court of the women's quarters, to learn of Esther's welfare and what was happening to her. Esther 2:9-11

As it turned out, Esther was chosen by the King to be his Queen.

> The king loved Esther more than all the *other* women, and she obtained grace and favor in his sight more than all the virgins; so he set the royal crown upon her head and made her queen instead of Vashti. Then the king made a great feast, the Feast of Esther, for all his officials and servants; and he proclaimed a holiday in the provinces and gave gifts according to the generosity of a king. Hmm..I guess that's favor. Esther 2:17,18

> After these things King Ahasuerus promoted Haman, and advanced him and set his seat above all the princes who *were* with him. And all the king's servants who *were* within the king's gate bowed and paid homage to Haman, for so the king had commanded concerning him. But Mordecai would not bow or pay homage. Esther 3:1-3

Mordecai would not bow to Haman. So Haman was very upset and was determined to have Mordecai hanged. And not only that, he decided to have all the people of Jewish descent killed.

Then Haman said to King Ahasuerus, "There is a certain people scattered and dispersed among the people in all the provinces of your kingdom; their laws *are* different from all *other* people, and they do not keep the king's laws. Therefore, it *is* not fitting for the king to let them remain. If it pleases the king, let *a decree* be written that they be destroyed, and I will pay ten thousand talents of silver into the hands of those who do the work, to bring *it* into the king's treasuries."

So the king took his signet ring from his hand and gave it to Haman, the son of Hammedatha the Agagite, the enemy of the Jews. And the king said to Haman, "The money and the people *are* given to you, to do with them as seems good to you. "Esther 3:8-11

Of course the King didn't know that Queen Esther was a Jew. So he agreed with Haman.

So Haman was very happy with everything the King had given him and was bragging about it to his Wife and friends but he said…

Yet all this avails me nothing, so long as I see Mordecai the Jew sitting at the king's gate."

Then his wife Zeresh and all his friends said to him "let a gallows be made, fifty cubits high, and in the morning suggest to the king that Mordecai be hanged on it; then go merrily with the king to the banquet." And the thing pleased Haman; so he had the gallows made. Esther 3:13,14

That night the king could not sleep. So one was commanded to bring the book of the records of the chronicles; and they were read before the king. And it was found written that Mordecai had told of Bigthana and Teresh, two of the king's eunuchs, the doorkeepers who had sought to lay hands on King Ahasuerus. Then the king said, "What honor or dignity has been bestowed on Mordecai for this? "And the king's servants who attended him said, "Nothing has been done for him." Esther 6:1-3

Now for some reason the King could not sleep, hmm, I wonder if God maybe was speaking to him? For some reason he also wanted to read in the book that had told about Mordecai saving the king from being killed by the two doorkeepers. No coincidence here, God heard the Jews' prayers and fasting, and was busy behind the scenes as usual.

So the king said, "Who *is* in the court?" Now Haman had *just* entered the outer court of the king's palace to suggest that the king hang Mordecai on the gallows that he had prepared for him.

The king's servants said to him, "Haman is there, standing in the court."

And the king said, "Let him come in."

So Haman came in, and the king asked him, "What shall be done for the man whom the king delights to honor?"

Now Haman thought in his heart, "Whom would the king delight to honor more than me?" And Haman answered the king, "*For* the man whom the king delights to honor, let a royal robe be brought which the king has worn, and a horse on which the king has ridden, which has a royal crest placed on its head. Then let this robe and horse be delivered to the hand of one of the king's most noble princes, that he may array the man whom the king delights to honor. Then parade him on horseback through the city square, and proclaim before him: 'Thus shall it be done to the man whom the king delights to honor!'"

Then the king said to Haman, "Hurry, take the robe and the horse, as you have suggested, and do so for Mordecai the Jew who sits within the king's gate! Leave nothing undone of all that you have spoken."

So Haman took the robe and the horse, arrayed Mordecai and led him on horseback through the city square, and proclaimed before him, "Thus shall it be done to the man whom the king delights to honor!"

So what in heaven's name is Haman going to do now?

Afterward Mordecai went back to the king's gate. But Haman hurried to his house, mourning and with his head covered. Esther 6:4-12

When Haman told his wife Zeresh and all his friends everything that had happened to him, his wise men and his wife Zeresh said to him, "If Mordecai, before whom you have begun to fall, is of Jewish descent, you will not prevail against him but will surely fall before him."

So, I guess they already knew that you don't mess with God's people.

Now to make matters worse, this obviously was not coincidence either, the meeting with Queen Esther right after the King read about Mordecai saving him, and the King honoring him via Haman.

When Queen Esther, Haman, and the King met, Queen Esther advised the King that she and all her people were to be put to death by Haman. The King initially was asking Queen Esther whatever her request was that it would be granted her, and her request was to have her people spared. Well it ended up that Haman was killed on the gallows that he prepared for Mordecai.

> **On that day King Ahasuerus gave Queen Esther the house of Haman, the enemy of the Jews. And Mordecai came before the king, for Esther had told how he *was related* to her. So the king took off his signet ring, which he had taken from Haman, and gave it to Mordecai; and Esther appointed Mordecai over the house of Haman. Esther 8:1,2**

> **So Mordecai went out from the presence of the king in royal apparel of blue and white, with a great crown of gold and a garment of fine linen and purple; and the city of Shushan rejoiced and was glad. Esther 8:15**

> **For Mordecai *was* great in the king's palace and his fame spread throughout all the provinces; for this man Mordecai became increasingly prominent. Thus the Jews defeated all their enemies with the stroke of the sword, with slaughter and destruction, and did what they pleased with those who hated them. Esther 9:4,5**

For Mordecai the Jew *was* second to King Ahasuerus, and was great among the Jews and well received by the multitude of his brethren, seeking the good of his people and speaking peace to all his countrymen. Esther 10:3

So, in this book there was overwhelming victory for the Jews, and Mordecai was basically given Haman's job, and honor. So here it is again, God saving and prospering his faithful people.

CHAPTER 14
JOB

This is the story of Job, and as many of you may know, he was blessed, largely by God. But then, catastrophe happened in his life and family, and it wasn't going too well for Job. But in the end God showed up and blessed Job twice as much as he had in the beginning.

> There was a man in the land of Uz, whose name *was* Job; and that man was blameless and upright, and one who feared God and shunned evil. And seven sons and three daughters were born to him. Also, his possessions were seven thousand sheep, three thousand camels, five hundred yoke of oxen, five hundred female donkeys, and a very large household, so that this man was the greatest of all the people of the East. Job 1:1-3

> Now there was a day when the sons of God came to present themselves before the LORD, and Satan also came among them. And the LORD said to Satan, "From where do you come?"

> So Satan answered the LORD and said, "From going to and fro on the earth, and from walking back and forth on it."

Then the LORD said to Satan, "Have you considered My Servant Job, that *there is* none like him on the earth, a blameless and upright man, one who fears God and shuns evil?"

So Satan answered the LORD and said, "Does Job fear God for nothing? Have You not made a hedge around him, around his household, and around all that he has on every side? You have blessed the work of his hands, and his possessions have increased in the land. But now, stretch out Your hand and touch all that he has, and he will surely curse You to Your face!"

And the LORD said to Satan, "Behold, all that he has *is* in your power; only do not lay a hand on his *person*."

So Satan went out from the presence of the LORD. Job 1:6-12

The Lord made a hedge about Job, and about his house, and about all that he had on every side. The Lord blessed the work of his hands, and his substance was increased in the land.

But then Satan came along and said, let's see if Job will still serve God if things are not going so well.

Job did lose everything and almost his life, before the Lord changed his circumstances, but Job remained faithful to the Lord. So, in conclusion, don't ever, ever give up, for in due time you will reap!

The Lord turned the captivity of Job when he prayed for his friends; also the Lord gave Job twice as much as he had before. Job 42 V10

Now the Lord blessed the latter *days* of Job more than his beginning; for he had fourteen thousand sheep, six thousand camels, one thousand yoke of oxen, and one thousand female donkeys. He also had seven sons and three daughters. In all the land were found no women *as* beautiful as the daughters of Job; and their father gave them an inheritance among their brothers.

After this Job lived one hundred and forty years, and saw his children and grandchildren *for* four generations. So Job died, old and full of days. Job 42:12-17

God made Job great, and wealthy, and blessed him and his family immensely.

CHAPTER 15
DANIEL

This is the story of Daniel, and his friends, and how they would not compromise their faith in God in any way and how God kept them, and honored and promoted them.

In the third year of the reign of Jehoiakim, king of Judah, came Nebuchandnezzar, king of Babylon, unto Jerusalem, and besieged it. Daniel 1:1

Then the king instructed Ashpenaz, the master of his eunuchs, to bring some of the children of Israel and some of the king's descendants and some of the nobles, young men in whom *there was* no blemish, but good-looking, gifted in all wisdom, possessing knowledge and quick to understand, who *had* ability to serve in the king's palace, and whom they might teach the language and literature of the Chaldeans. And the king appointed for them a daily provision of the king's delicacies and of the wine which he drank, and three years of training for them, so that at the end of *that time* they might serve before the king. Now from among those of the sons of Judah were Daniel, Hananiah, Mishael, and Azariah. To them

the chief of the eunuchs gave names: he gave Daniel *the name* Belteshazzar; to Hananiah, Shadrach; to Mishael, Meshach; and to Azariah, Abed-Nego.

But Daniel purposed in his heart that he would not defile himself with the portion of the king's delicacies, nor with the wine which he drank; therefore, he requested of the chief of the eunuchs that he might not defile himself. Now God had brought Daniel into the favor and goodwill of the chief of the eunuchs. And the chief of the eunuchs said to Daniel, "I fear my lord the king, who has appointed your food and drink. For why should he see your faces looking worse than the young men who *are* your age? Then you would endanger my head before the king."

So Daniel said to the steward whom the chief of the eunuchs had set over Daniel, Hananiah, Mishael, and Azariah, "Please test your servants for ten days, and let them give us vegetables to eat and water to drink. Then let our appearance be examined before you, and the appearance of the young men who eat the portion of the king's delicacies; and as you see fit, *so* deal with your servants." So he consented with them in this matter, and tested them ten days.

And at the end of ten days their features appeared better and fatter in flesh than all the young men who ate the portion of the king's delicacies. Thus the steward took away their portion of delicacies and the wine that they were to drink, and gave them vegetables.

As for these four young men, God gave them knowledge and skill in all literature and wisdom;

and Daniel had understanding in all visions and dreams.

Now at the end of the days, when the king had said that they should be brought in, the chief of the eunuchs brought them in before Nebuchadnezzar. Then the king interviewed them, and among them all none was found like Daniel, Hananiah, Mishael, and Azariah; therefore, they served before the king. And in all matters of wisdom *and* understanding about which the king examined them, he found them ten times better than all the magicians *and* astrologers who *were* in all his realm. Thus Daniel continued until the first year of King Cyrus. Daniel 1:4-21

Hmm…I guess it's worth it to serve and obey God.

Nebuchadnezzer, in the second year of his reign, had dreamed a dream and his spirit was troubled, and his sleep went from him. He called for all the magicians, astrologers, the sorcerers, and the Chaldeans. Not any of them could tell him the dream and the interpretation.

The Chaldeans answered the king, and said, "There is not a man on earth who can tell the king's matter; therefore no king, lord, or ruler has *ever* asked such things of any magician, astrologer, or Chaldean. *It is* a difficult thing that the king requests, and there is no other who can tell it to the king except the gods, whose dwelling is not with flesh. "Daniel 2:10,11

For this reason, the king was angry and very furious, and gave the command to destroy all the wise *men* of Babylon. So the decree went out, and they began killing the wise *men*; and they sought Daniel and his companions, to kill them. Daniel 2:12,13

So Daniel went in and asked the king to give him time, that he might tell the king the interpretation. Then Daniel went to his house, and made the decision known to Hananiah, Mishael, and Azariah, his companions, that they might seek mercies from the God of heaven concerning this secret, so that Daniel and his companions might not perish with the rest of the wise *men* of Babylon. Then the secret was revealed to Daniel in a night vision. So Daniel blessed the God of heaven.

Daniel answered and said:
"Blessed be the name of God forever and ever,
for wisdom and might are His.
And He changes the times and the seasons;
He removes kings and raises up kings;
He gives wisdom to the wise
and knowledge to those who have understanding.
He reveals deep and secret things;
He knows what *is* in the darkness,
and light dwells with Him.

"I thank You and praise You,
O God of my fathers;
You have given me wisdom and might,
And have now made known to me what we asked of You,
For You have made known to us the king's demand."

Daniel answered in the presence of the king, and said, "The secret which the king has demanded, the wise *men*, the astrologers, the magicians, and the soothsayers cannot declare to the king. But there is a God in heaven who reveals secrets, and He has made known to King Nebuchadnezzar what will be in the latter days. Daniel 2:16-28

Then Daniel proceeded to share with the king all that the Lord had revealed to him.

Then King Nebuchadnezzar threw himself down before Daniel and worshiped him, and he commanded his people to offer sacrifices and burn sweet incense before him. The king said to Daniel, "Truly, your God is the greatest of gods, the Lord over kings, a revealer of mysteries, for you have been able to reveal this secret."

Then the king appointed Daniel to a high position and gave him many valuable gifts. He made Daniel ruler over the whole province of Babylon, as well as chief over all his wise men. At Daniel's request, the king appointed Shadrach, Meshach, and Abednego to be in charge of all the affairs of the province of Babylon, while Daniel remained in the king's court. Daniel 2:46-49

Wow! God is good!

SHADRACH, MESHACH, AND ABEDNEGO

This story is about the three youths Shadrach, Meshach, and Abednego who would not conform to the world and the King, who wanted them to bow down and worship a golden image. They stayed faithful to the Lord God and God rewarded them.

Therefore at that time certain Chaldeans came forward and accused the Jews. They spoke and said to King Nebuchadnezzar, "O king, live forever! You, O king, have made a decree that everyone who hears the sound of the horn, flute, harp, lyre, *and* psaltery, in symphony with all kinds of music, shall fall down and worship the gold image; and whoever does not fall down and worship shall be cast into the midst of a burning fiery furnace. There are certain Jews whom you have set over the affairs of the province of Babylon: Shadrach, Meshach, and Abed-Nego; these men, O king, have not paid due regard to you. They do not serve your gods or worship the gold image which you have set up."

Then Nebuchadnezzar, in rage and fury, gave the command to bring Shadrach, Meshach, and Abed-Nego. So they brought these men before the king. Nebuchadnezzar spoke, saying to them, "*Is it* true, Shadrach, Meshach, and Abed-Nego, *that* you do not serve my gods or worship the gold image which I have set up? Now if you are ready at the time you hear the sound of the horn, flute, harp, lyre, *and* psaltery, in symphony with all kinds of music, and you fall down and worship the image which I have made, *good!* But if you do not worship, you shall be cast immediately into the midst of a burning fiery furnace. And who *is* the god who will deliver you from my hands?"

Shadrach, Meshach, and Abed-Nego answered and said to the king, "O Nebuchadnezzar, we have no need to answer you in this matter. If that *is the case,* our God whom we serve is able to deliver us from the burning fiery furnace, and He will deliver *us* from your hand, O king. But if not, let it be known to you, O king, that we do not serve your gods, nor will we worship the gold image which you have set up."

SAVED IN FIERY TRIAL

Then Nebuchadnezzar was full of fury, and the expression on his face changed toward Shadrach, Meshach, and Abed-Nego. He spoke and commanded that they heat the furnace seven times more than it was usually heated. And he commanded certain mighty men of valor who *were* in his army to bind Shadrach, Meshach, and Abed-Nego, *and* cast *them* into the burning fiery furnace. Then these men were bound in their coats, their trousers, their turbans, and their *other* garments, and were cast into the midst of the burning fiery furnace. Therefore, because the king's command was urgent, and the furnace exceedingly hot, the flame of the fire killed those men who took up Shadrach, Meshach, and Abed-Nego. And these three men, Shadrach, Meshach, and Abed-Nego, fell down bound into the midst of the burning fiery furnace.

Then King Nebuchadnezzar was astonished; and he rose in haste *and* spoke, saying to his counselors, "Did we not cast three men bound into the midst of the fire?"

They answered and said to the king, "True, O king."

"Look!" he answered, "I see four men loose, walking in the midst of the fire; and they are not hurt, and the form of the fourth is like the Son of God."

NEBUCHADNEZZAR PRAISES GOD

Then Nebuchadnezzar went near the mouth of the burning fiery furnace *and* spoke, saying, "Shadrach, Meshach, and Abed-Nego, servants of the Most High God, come out, and come *here*." Then Shadrach, Meshach, and Abed-Nego came from the midst of the fire. And the satraps, administrators, governors, and the king's counselors gathered together, and they saw these men on whose bodies the fire had no power; the hair of their head was not singed nor were their garments affected, and the smell of fire was not on them.

Nebuchadnezzar spoke, saying, "Blessed be the God of Shadrach, Meshach, and Abed-Nego, who sent His Angel and delivered His servants who trusted in Him, and they have frustrated the king's word, and yielded their bodies, that they should not serve nor worship any god except their own God! Therefore I make a decree that any people, nation, or language which speaks anything amiss against the God of Shadrach, Meshach, and Abed-Nego shall be cut in pieces, and their houses shall be made an ash heap; because there is no other God who can deliver like this."

Then the king promoted Shadrach, Meshach, and Abed-Nego in the province of Babylon. Daniel 3:8-30

Then the king promoted Shadrach, Meshach, and Abednego to even higher positions in the province of Babylon.

I guess that sounds like they had pretty much anything that they wanted or needed.

Shadrach, Meshach and Abednego would not compromise and serve any other Gods' but the Lord God Almighty. God delivered them and promoted them!

DANIEL IN THE LION'S DEN

Now, most of us know the story of Daniel and the lion's den.

Darius the Mede set one hundred and twenty princes over the kingdom. Three presidents were set over the princes, of whom Daniel was first.

> **Daniel was preferred above the presidents and princes, because an excellent spirit was in him; and the King sought to set him over the whole realm. Daniel 6:3**

The presidents and princes obviously didn't like that idea so they tried to find fault in Daniel, but Daniel was faithful and they could not find any error in him. Then they said that we cannot find any occasion against him except regarding the law of his God. They all decided to establish a royal statute, that whosoever shall ask a petition of any God besides King Darius for thirty days, shall be cast into the lion's den. They then went to King Darius and asked him to establish and sign the decree, and he did.

When Daniel knew that the decree was signed, he went into his house with his windows open and kneeled down three times a day to pray to God and thank Him, just as he usually did.

The men saw Daniel praying and went to the King to tell him that Daniel was praying to his God. When the King found this out he was very displeased and upset with himself, and set out to deliver

Daniel. They brought Daniel to him and he said to Daniel, your God whom you serve continually, he will deliver you. They then cast him into the den of lion's. The King went to his palace and fasted all night. He then got up very early and went in haste to the den of lions. He cried into the den and asked Daniel if his God was able to deliver him. Daniel said that God sent an angel to shut the lion's mouths and there was no fault found in him. He was exceedingly glad for Daniel and he was taken out of the den. And the men who accused Daniel were thrown into the den with their families, and the lions ate them up before they reached the bottom of the den. Ouch! It is probably best not to mess with a man of God.

> **Then King Darius sent this message to the people of every race and nation and language throughout the world:**
>
> **"I decree that everyone throughout my kingdom should tremble with fear before the God of Daniel.**
>
> **For he is the living God,**
> **and he will endure forever.**
> **His kingdom will never be destroyed,**
> **and his rule will never end.**
> **He rescues and saves his people;**
> **he performs miraculous signs and wonders**
> **in the heavens and on earth.**
> **He has rescued Daniel**
> **from the power of the lions.**
>
> **"So Daniel prospered during the reign of Darius and the reign of Cyrus the Persian. Daniel 6:25-28**

Daniel was always getting promoted and exalted in the Kingdom of Babylon. Daniel prospered during the reign of all the kings he was under. The reason was because he had an excellent spirit and was faithful to God. God blessed him with wisdom and understanding of dreams and visions, which brought him much favor. Again he was basically one of the highest rulers of the Kingdom most of the time, and he was originally a captive of Babylon. God can truly turn any unfortunate circumstance around!

CHAPTER 16
JESUS

Many people would say that Jesus was not necessarily rich with an abundance of money. But, if you noticed, Jesus had everything that He wanted and everything that He needed. Jesus prayed and God answered. He had the favor of God, which meant whatever He wanted or needed it was there. He prospered in every area. I know we are just talking about finances, but Jesus, as far as the bible says, and I can see, didn't really lack for anything. His Ministry had a finance man with a money bag and Judas handling it (reference John 12:6, John 13:29). He needed to pay taxes and He told Peter to go fishing and the money would be in the fish's mouth and it was, and even the correct amount. Math 17:24

The first miracle recorded in the bible that Jesus performed was a miracle of provision, the wine ran out at a wedding feast and obviously they didn't have the money or resources to go out and get more, because Jesus wouldn't have had to step in.

Jesus and his family and disciples were invited to a wedding, and the wine ran out. So, while they were considering what to do about it, Mary asked Jesus if He could help. He said no Mother it is not my time yet. She acted like she didn't hear Him and she told the servants to do what He said. So he told them to fill the pots with water and bring them to the master of the wedding. He took a drink and said to the bridegroom that it was wonderful that they saved the best wine for last, usually the best wine was used first and then later in the evening the lesser wine was brought. There you have it, Jesus' first miracle, I am not really sure it was a need, but God answers prayers. John 2:1

When Jesus had heard about John's death, He went out to a desert place privately. A multitude of people followed Him and when Jesus saw them he was moved with compassion and healed their sick. When evening was setting in, the disciples came to Him and told him it was getting late and wondered if they should send the people away to the villages in the area to get food. Jesus told the disciples that they need not to depart and to go ahead and feed them. The disciples replied that they had only five loaves of bread and two fishes.

Jesus told the disciples to bring the food to Him and he commanded the people to sit down on the grass, and took the five loaves, and two fishes and looking up to heaven, He blessed and broke and gave the loaves to his disciples, and the disciples gave them to the people. All the people ate and were filled, and when they took up the leftovers, there were twelve baskets full left! Whoa, that's a lot of leftovers! And then the bible says that there were about five thousand men, not even including the woman and children. Matthew 14:13-21

After Jesus' death, Peter and some of the disciples decided to go fishing. They fished all night and caught nothing. In the morning they saw someone standing on the shore which was Jesus. He asked them if they had anything to eat. They said no we have been fishing all night and have caught nothing. Jesus told them to cast their net on the right side of the boat and they will catch some. They caught so many fish that they were not able to draw it in. The Bible says that the net didn't even break and there were 153 large fish. So now they had enough fish for breakfast! John 21:1

So now we know that Jesus can produce wine for a wedding, taxes for the year, overflowing fish for a business, food for over five thousand people, and remember we are just talking about provision! Does He qualify as being rich? A person without finances couldn't do any of this, unless of course he knows the Master!

Chapter 17
The Offering

The offering is about the men and woman that I have spoken of in the preceding chapters and the offerings that they have given to God. It is very interesting how in the Old Testament the offering many times was a burnt offering, meaning they would burn the animal they were offering to God, and at times a large amount of them. And if they had very large herds, that more than likely represented greatness and wealth. Nobody really benefited in the natural from this giving act to God, you would think. But to God it was very important to see how much a person truly honored and loved Him.

There is also the example of the building of the Temple of Solomon, how David gave largely and all the people joined in and gave so much so that they had to tell them to stop they had so much. This would be like giving towards the building of a church today, the building fund of the church that maybe a person would be attending.

In this day and age, it is a bit different than giving a burnt offering to the Lord. There are times when God is saying to give to this ministry or give to that person a certain amount of money or material item.

Or again, a Minister is preaching about giving and people might say that he is just asking for money again, oh brother! But in reality He is being led by God to teach the people to learn how to give for their benefit not necessarily for the benefit of the speaker, because it is really about Giving to God and the givers heart, not about the speaker needing money. Now yes, of course the Minister needs the money, and the Bible does say to bring all the tithes to the storehouse, and to give to Ministers what is due them, but God will get the money to them one way or another. Giving of the offering is also about the giver and his commitment to God, and how God will bless him by doing it.

ABRAHAM--

There was a war in the land and Lot who was living in Sodom and Gomorrah was taken captive along with others and all their goods. Abram and all his men went after them and rescued them and took them back home along with all the goods. Melchizedek the King of Salem, who was the priest of the most high God, met them as they returned and blessed Abram, and Abram gave him tithes of all.

Now just after Abram did this, God said to him in a vision; Fear not Abram, I am thy shield and thy exceeding great reward. Exceeding great reward, sounds really good, doesn't it? I really do not think it was coincidental that God revealed Himself to Abram just after he gave an offering to Melchizedek, and told him He was his reward, His exceedingly great reward!

ABRAHAM AND ISAAC--

God spoke to Abraham to test him and told him to offer up his son, his only son Isaac as a burnt offering to the Lord. Hmm..quite an offering. Abraham and Sarah's miracle promise was finally manifest after about 25 years of waiting, and then God tests Abraham to see if he is willing to give up the promise and obey God.

Just as Abraham was about to kill Isaac, an Angel of the Lord called to him out of heaven and said, Abraham, lay not thy hand upon the lad, for now I know that you fear God, seeing that you have not withheld your only son from me. And when Abraham looked up he saw a ram caught in the thicket by his horns and took the ram for a burnt offering to the Lord.

Again, after Abraham sowed this offering and was actually going to sacrifice his son, the Lord spoke to him again and said He would bless him, and multiply him, and in thy seed shall all the nations of the earth be blessed, and your seed will possess the gate of their enemies, because you have obeyed my voice. Genesis 22:1-18

ISAAC--

Here is an example of Isaac blessing God when the Lord appeared to him in Beersheba and said fear not, for I am with thee, and I will bless thee, and multiply thy seed for my servant Abraham's sake. And he built an altar there and called upon the name of the Lord. Genesis 26:23-25

JACOB--

> Then God said to Jacob, "Arise, go up to Bethel and dwell there; and make an altar there to God, who appeared to you when you fled from the face of Esau your brother."Genesis 35:1

> Then God appeared to Jacob again, when he came from Padan Aram, and blessed him. And God said to him, "Your name *is* Jacob; your name shall not be called Jacob anymore, but Israel shall be your name." So He called his name Israel. Also God said to him: "I *am* God Almighty. Be fruitful and multiply; a nation and a company of nations shall proceed from you, and kings shall come from your body. The land which I gave Abraham and Isaac I give to you; and to your descendants after you I give this land." Then God went up from him in the place

where He talked with him. So Jacob set up a pillar in the place where He talked with him, a pillar of stone; and he poured a drink offering on it, and he poured oil on it. And Jacob called the name of the place where God spoke with him, Bethel. Genesis 35:9-15

Here we see an example of a drink offering. The Bible doesn't say too much about drink offerings, but nevertheless it was an offering to God. An offering can be anything that is of any value to the person giving it, or whatever God wants or asks of that person.

JOSHUA--

The Lord told Joshua to take the city of AI and he obeyed and took all the cattle and spoil. Then Joshua built an altar to the Lord in mount Ebal, in accordance with the command of Moses. Joshua 8:30-35

RUTH--

Ruth gave up her life and her hometown for the Lord and Naomi, and was rewarded for it.

HANNAH--

Hannah and her Husband would go up to Shiloh every year to sacrifice and worship to the Lord, Her husband would always give Hannah a wealthy portion because she had no children and his other wife did. The Lord saw their faithfulness of giving and worshiping so He blessed them with what they were asking for, which was children.

Now Hannah actually did sacrifice her first son Samuel and gave him to the church at a very young age, as soon as he was weaned. She promised the Lord that if He gave her a child she would give him to the Lord and she did. Then she was blessed with five children after Samuel. Samuel went on to be a great prophet.

THE WIDOW AND ELIJAH--

The widow gave a portion of the last meal she had to Elijah in obedience to the Lord. Now in this day and age the Prophet or Minister would probably be marked as a mooch by the press and everyone else, not knowing what the Lord was doing of course. But when she gave that offering to the man of God, the Lord multiplied it, and she was able to continue to live on it, her family and Elijah, until the famine subsided.

HEZEKIAH--

Not only did Hezekiah and his congregation offer peace and burnt offerings to the Lord, but he and his leaders also gave to the assembly thousands of bulls and sheep. And the Lord heard Hezekiah's prayer and healed the people. Their voice was heard and their prayers came up to His holy dwelling place, to heaven.

Moreover, he commanded the people who dwelt in Jerusalem to contribute support for the priests and the Levites, that they might devote themselves to the Law of the LORD.

> **As soon as the commandment was circulated, the children of Israel brought in abundance the first fruits of grain and wine, oil and honey, and of all the produce of the field; and they brought in abundantly the tithe of everything. And the children of Israel and Judah, who dwelt in the cities of Judah, brought the tithe of oxen and sheep; also the tithe of holy things which were consecrated to the LORD their God, they laid it in heaps.**

In the third month they began laying them in heaps, and they finished in the seventh month. And when Hezekiah and the leaders came and saw the heaps, they blessed the LORD and His people Israel. Then Hezekiah questioned the priests and the Levites concerning the heaps. And Azariah the chief priest, from the house of Zadok, answered him and said, "Since *the people* began to bring the offerings into the house of the LORD, we have had enough to eat and have plenty left, for the LORD has blessed His people; and what is left *is* this great abundance. 2 Chronicles 31:4-10

The people gave so much that there was great abundance left over for the house of the Lord. For the Lord blessed the people. He blessed the people so they could give generously!

DAVID--

Here is an example of some of the offerings that David made to the Lord.

So they brought the ark of the LORD, and set it in its place in the midst of the tabernacle that David had erected for it. Then David offered burnt offerings and peace offerings before the LORD. 2 Samuel 6:17

Then the king said to Araunah, "No, but I will surely buy it from you for a price; nor will I offer burnt offerings to the LORD my God with that which costs me nothing." So David bought the threshing floor and the oxen for fifty shekels of silver. 2 Samuel 24:23

Wow, David was not willing to sacrifice anything to the Lord that was given to him, or that would cost him nothing, wanting the sacrifice to be worth something and really be a sacrifice.

> **And David built there an altar to the LORD, and offered burnt offerings and peace offerings. So the LORD heeded the prayers for the land, and the plague was withdrawn from Israel. 2 Samuel 24:24,25**

The Lord heard David's prayer after he offered burnt offerings and peace offerings to the Lord and the plague was withdrawn from Israel.

> **And David built there an altar to the LORD, and offered burnt offerings and peace offerings, and called on the LORD; and He answered him from heaven by fire on the altar of burnt offering. 1 Chronicles 21:25**

The Lord answered him by sending fire for the offering!!

> **Now David said, "Solomon my son *is* young and inexperienced, and the house to be built for the LORD *must be* exceedingly magnificent, famous and glorious throughout all countries. I will now make preparation for it." So David made abundant preparations before his death. 1 Chronicles 22:5**

David wanted to make sure the Lord had the most beautiful house in all the land! And everyone would see and know it.

David gave largely to build the temple for the Lord, as we spoke about in the previous chapter on David. It was well over a billion dollars that he gave towards the building of the Temple. Now that is an offering!

SOLOMON--

Solomon made many offerings to the Lord;

> Now the king went to Gibeon to sacrifice there, for that *was* the great high place: Solomon offered a thousand burnt offerings on that altar. At Gibeon the LORD appeared to Solomon in a dream by night; and God said, "Ask! What shall I give you?" 1 Kings 3:4,5

After Solomon offered his sacrifice the Lord wanted to bless him and said what can I give you?

> So if you walk in My ways, to keep My statutes and My commandments, as your father David walked, then I will lengthen your days." Then Solomon awoke; and indeed it had been a dream. And he came to Jerusalem and stood before the ark of the covenant of the LORD, offered up burnt offerings, offered peace offerings, and made a feast for all his servants. 1 Kings 3:14,15

> Then the king and all Israel with him offered sacrifices before the LORD. And Solomon offered a sacrifice of peace offerings, which he offered to the LORD, twenty-two thousand bulls and one hundred and twenty thousand sheep. So the king and all the children of Israel dedicated the house of the LORD. On the same day the king consecrated the middle of the court that *was* in front of the house of the LORD; for there he offered burnt offerings, grain offerings, and the fat of the peace offerings, because the bronze altar that *was* before the LORD *was* too small to receive the burnt offerings, the

grain offerings, and the fat of the peace offerings. 1 Kings 8:63,64

Now three times a year Solomon offered burnt offerings and peace offerings on the altar which he had built for the LORD, and he burned incense with them on the altar that was before the LORD. So he finished the temple. 1 Kings 9:25

[Solomon Anointed King] And they made sacrifices to the LORD and offered burnt offerings to the LORD on the next day: a thousand bulls, a thousand rams, a thousand lambs, with their drink offerings, and sacrifices in abundance for all Israel. 1 Chronicles 29:21

And Solomon went up there to the bronze altar before the LORD, which was at the tabernacle of meeting, and offered a thousand burnt offerings on it. 2 Chronicles 1:6

[Solomon Dedicates the Temple] When Solomon had finished praying, fire came down from heaven and consumed the burnt offering and the sacrifices; and the glory of the LORD filled the temple. 2 Chronicles 7:1

Furthermore Solomon consecrated the middle of the court that was in front of the house of the LORD; for there he offered burnt offerings and the fat of the peace offerings, because the bronze altar which Solomon had made was not able to receive the burnt offerings, the grain offerings, and the fat. 2 Chronicles 7:7

It seems Solomon was a big giver like his father, David.

ESTHER--

The Book of Esther shows the Jews crying out to God in the form of fasting and praying for three days, when they were informed of their annihilation. Then once the Jews were saved from destruction and had the victory over their enemies, they made an annual feast celebration called Purim to remember and celebrate the victory they had. In this celebration they give gifts to one another and to the poor. This also is a form of offering to the Lord by giving.

JOB--

Job regularly went and sanctified his sons and offered burnt offerings for each one of his children after the end of their feasts. Saying that, it may be that my sons have sinned and cursed God in their hearts, and Job did this continually.

DANIEL--

Daniel offered up to the Lord; prayer, supplication and fasting many times throughout the Book of Daniel.

> **Then I set my face toward the Lord God to make request by prayer and supplications, with fasting, sackcloth, and ashes. And I prayed to the LORD my God, and made confession, and said, "O Lord, great and awesome God, who keeps His covenant and mercy with those who love Him, and with those who keep His commandments, we have sinned and committed iniquity, we have done wickedly and rebelled, even by departing from Your precepts and Your judgments. Daniel 9:3-5**

CORNELIUS ACTS 10--

> There was a certain man in Caesarea called
> Cornelius, a centurion of what was called the Italian
> Regiment, a devout *man* and one who feared God
> with all his household, who gave alms generously to
> the people, and prayed to God always.

The meaning in the Greek for alms is generosity to the poor.
Cornelius gave generously to the poor and to the Lord.

> About the ninth hour of the day he saw clearly in
> a vision an angel of God coming in and saying to
> him, "Cornelius!" And when he observed him, he
> was afraid, and said, "What is it, lord?" Acts 10:1-4

So he said to him, "Your prayers and your alms have come up
for a memorial before God. Oh my, God is saying that an offering
of a sweet aroma has come up before Him, that is, his prayers and
giving got God's attention. The bible goes on to say that Peter was
sent by God to his house to preach about Jesus and salvation, and
the power of God fell on them all and they were given the gift of
the Holy Spirit and spoke with other tongues and magnified God.
Now this was even more of a miracle because Cornelius and his
household were gentiles. So the Jews were finding out that God
wanted everyone to be blessed with salvation and the gift of the
Holy Spirit. So, start giving generously and God will bless you back.
In this situation it wasn't necessarily finances, but this was much
better than finances, Cornelius and his household were saved and
filled with the Holy Spirit! The greatest of all miracles! And I am
sure that Cornelius was also well taken care of by his giving much
alms to the poor. And oh, by the way, don't forget to pray! God
always likes to hear from you.

JESUS--

Jesus gave the most important sacrifice of all, himself. With His sacrifice the whole world was affected and never again would have to offer sacrifices of bulls and goats, or animals, to pay for their sins. Jesus did it once and for all for anyone who will accept Him. For God so loved the world that he gave His only begotten son, that who so ever shall believe in Him shall be forgiven with remission of sins and have eternal life!

CHAPTER 18
THE CHARACTER

Are you willing and obedient? These people were....

Abraham--Faithful, full of faith, and righteous.

And he believed in the LORD, and it was accounted it to him for righteousness. Abraham had great faith in God. First his son being born when he and his wife were way beyond child bearing years, he continued to believe God even when it didn't happen for many years. Then, when the Lord asked him to sacrifice his son he still had faith that somehow the Lord would make a way for him to be the father of many nations.

> **Who, contrary to hope, in hope believed, so that he became the father of many nations, according to what was spoken, "So shall your descendants be." And not being weak in faith, he did not consider his own body, already dead (since he was about a hundred years old), and the deadness of Sarah's womb. He did not waver at the promise of God through unbelief, but was strengthened in faith, giving glory to God, and being fully convinced that what He had promised He was also able to perform. And therefore it was accounted to him for righteousness. Romans 4:18-22**

Isaac--Believed and trusted God. There was a famine in the land and the Lord told Isaac not to go down to Egypt but to the land that I will tell you to go. Isaac sowed in that land and received in the same year a hundred fold return. Isaac believed and trusted in God and was blessed.

Jacob--Endured, Jacob struggled with God and man, and prevailed. Jacob would not let God go until he blessed him. Jacob said, I have seen God face to face and my life is preserved.

Joseph-- Stayed faithful and didn't compromise, he had integrity, he was a goodly person the bible says, which means handsome, and he had wisdom and understanding.

Joshua--Joshua was a good leader, courageous and confident in the Lord, and a successful warrior.

Ruth--Faithful, and hard working.

Hannah--Desperate, thankful and faithful, and had integrity when she did what she told the Lord she would do in giving her son to the church and the Lord.

Hezekiah--

> **Thus Hezekiah did throughout all Judah, and he did what *was* good and right and true before the Lord his God. And in every work that he began in the service of the house of God, in the law and in the commandment, to seek his God, he did *it* with all his heart. So he prospered. 2 Chronicles 31:20, 21**

Everything he did for the Lord he did with all his heart.

David-- Faithful, believed in and trusted in the Lord, courageous, loved the Lord, was a warrior, and committed to the Lord. 'I have found David the *son* of Jesse, a man after My *own* heart, who will do all My will. From this man's seed, according to *the* promise, God raised up for Israel a Savior—Jesus. Acts 13:23

Solomon--God gave Solomon wisdom and exceeding much understanding, and largeness of heart, even as the sand that is on the seashore. Solomon's heart was just to lead the people fairly, and God blessed him with much, much more because that was all he asked for.

> **And Solomon's wisdom excelled the wisdom of all the children of the east country and all the wisdom of Egypt. His fame was in all regions round about. He spoke three thousand proverbs, and his songs were a thousand and five. And there came from all people to hear the wisdom of Solomon, from all kings of the earth, who had heard of his wisdom. 1kings 4:29-34**

Esther--Was faithful and willing to die for her people and nation. She prayed and fasted.

Mordicai--Was faithful and would not bow down to Haman. He prayed and fasted. He was Very courageous.

Job--Perfect and upright, he feared the Lord and shunned evil. He stayed faithful even through the most trying circumstances.

Daniel--Had an excellent spirit, was very faithful and loved the Lord, he would not defile himself, and he had self control. He was courageous, with wisdom and understanding. Always praying to the Lord and fasting.

Cornelius---A devout man, and feared God, he was a giving man, and prayed to God always.

Jesus--Said of Himself, that He was meek and lowly in heart. He did only those things he saw His Father do, and to please the Father and not himself. He said he was only here to do the will of God. He stayed faithful to die for the world. The Bible says He humbled Himself, and became obedient unto death, even the death of the cross. He wasn't afraid of the religious leaders; he spoke with authority and power, and never backed off. He did the works of the Father's heart, by healing the oppressed and making disciples of men.

CHAPTER 19
CHARACTERISTICS SUMMARY

Faithful, obedient, committed, spirit of excellence, willing to do all God's will, largeness of heart, did everything with all his heart, trusted in the Lord, courageous, not fearful, good and right and true, loved God, sought out the Lord, meek and lowly in heart, willing to give up his life, do the works of the Lord, devout, fear of the Lord, giving, a pray-er, fasted, perfect and upright, full of integrity, hard working, self controlled, believed God and was counted as righteousness, confident in the Lord, will endure to the end, having wisdom and understanding.

These are just some of the characteristics that have come from this study. It seems kind of overwhelming, doesn't it?

Staying hooked to the vine is first and foremost really. What I mean by that is first of all receiving Jesus as your personal Lord and savior, and committing your life to Him. Then making sure that you stay hooked to the vine and consistently taking in the gospel, reading the Bible, finding a bible based church that is reaching out to the lost and poor. Giving of your tithes and offerings consistently. As you are doing that the Lord will lead you and guide you and give you wisdom to fulfill His plan for your life. His plans are good for you and will always keep you going and expecting.

> **For I know the plans I have for you, declares the Lord, plans to prosper you and not to harm you, plans to give you a hope and a future. Jeremiah 29:11**

And He doesn't lie. So you can believe it and expect it.

PRAYER OF SALVATION

If you haven't asked Jesus into your heart and would like to dedicate your life to Him, I would like to give you the opportunity to do so now. Just say this prayer out loud to the Lord;

Dear Lord Jesus, come into my heart, be my Lord and savior, forgive me of my sins, set me free. I believe that Jesus died on the cross for me and my sins, was raised from the dead and is coming back again very soon. I am saved and forgiven and on my way to heaven because I have Jesus in my heart.

Yeah!! If you prayed that prayer this will start you on the most wonderful journey you have ever been on, because the Lord loves you very much and has a wonderful plan for your life.

CHAPTER 20
RELATED SCRIPTURES

The thief does not come except to steal, and to kill, and to destroy. I have come that they may have life, and that they may have *it* more abundantly. John 10:10

There is *one* who scatters, yet increases more; and there is *one* who withholds more than is right, but it *leads* to poverty. The generous soul will be made rich, and he who waters will also be watered himself. Proverbs 11:24,25

He who has a slack hand becomes poor, but the hand of the diligent makes rich. Proverbs 10:4

This Book of the Law shall not depart from your mouth, but you shall meditate in it day and night, that you may observe to do according to all that is written in it. For then you will make your way prosperous, and then you will have good success. Joshua 1:8

Bring all the tithes into the storehouse, that there may be food in My house, and try Me now in this," Says the Lord of hosts, "If I will not open for you the windows of heaven and pour out for you *such* blessing that *there will* not *be room* enough *to receive it.* Malachi 3:10

Honor the LORD with your possessions, and with the first fruits of all your increase; so your barns will be filled with plenty, and your vats will overflow with new wine. Proverbs 3:10

Printed in the United States
by Baker & Taylor Publisher Services